DON'T JUST HAVE THE SOUP

DON'T JUST HAVE THE SOUP

52 ANALOGIES *for* LEADERSHIP, COACHING *and* LIFE

Alan Heymann

Illustrations by
Lindy Russell-Heymann

Cover art by Dennis Samson

Printed in the United States of America

First Printing, 2021

ISBN 9780578305998

Peaceful Direction
2703 Dennis Ave
Silver Spring, MD 20902

thesoupbook.com

Contents

Introduction

Why a collection of analogies?

The world's cup runneth over with books about leadership and coaching. You'll find tens of thousands of these at your favorite online megastore, and I've probably read a couple hundred myself. Some are by the world's best thinkers in the field, who bring their extensive educational background and work experience into their scholarship. Many of these books fall along two lines: a new model for how our minds work and how to change our behavior, or a deep dive into a particular subject (like delegation, prioritization or spending less time on your email).

What you have in your hands is not one of those books.

I am not an expert in any one given thing, nor do my talents extend to researching a thing thoroughly enough to write a book about it. What I am is an avid collector of stories. Since beginning my career as a television journalist a quarter century ago, I've come to know that humans make meaning in their lives through stories. As an executive coach, I help my clients unpack and see through their own stories, achieving more success as a result.

The frame of a story matters. I've found that reframing is one of the most powerful tools in the practice of coaching. The process of meeting clients where they are, of reframing their thoughts around a universal or familiar story, has made me a more effective coach. Analogies are a simple way to weave that story together. Sometimes, analogies come to me in the middle of a coaching conversation. Sometimes, clients throw their own analogies into the mix. I've picked up a few from other coaches along the way as well.

What you're about to read is a collection of 52 analogies for coaching, leadership and life. They're organized around 6 topics:

- **The leader mindset**
- **Communication**
- **Time and attention**
- **Relationships**
- **Transitions**
- **Coaching**

Lastly, here's a quick note on how this book might be useful. You could read it cover to cover. You could read one analogy a week for a whole year. And it's small enough to keep on your shelf as a reference when a story might be useful in helping you reframe something in your own life. I'd encourage you to bookmark these pages, make notes in them — or even order an extra copy to cut out the illustrations and post them around your office.

Why the soup?

Lindy and I had a few ideas for the title of this book, all of which came from the collection of analogies. A couple of them seemed especially strong. Then along came Dennis Samson, a talented designer I've known for more than a decade. Dennis was working on the cover art and threw one of my own analogies back at me! He was looking for a file in a particular format, and wrote that he was "about to accept the soup" before he decided to ask again for what he really needed.

We've all heard stories of people who seem to bend the world to their will, rather than the other way around. I'm thinking about the leader with the Diet Coke button under his desk, or the band that expects the post-concert bowl of M&Ms with all of the green ones removed. I imagine it must be disappointing when not everything ends up just so.

But some of us mere mortals wind up disappointed when someone or something doesn't meet our expectations *because we haven't made those expectations clear*. As you'll read, accepting the soup is about settling for something that falls short of what we need.

Please don't just have the soup.

Alan Heymann
Montgomery County, Maryland
November 2021

SECTION 1

⤳

The Leader Mindset

I n coach training at Georgetown University, we learned to coach the entire client. This means encouraging our clients to notice and understand what is going on in the body and the spirit in addition to the mind. Indeed, knowledge workers can always use a reminder that the body isn't just a sack of meat that carries our brains around.

Still, leadership coaches aren't doctors and we're not clergy. We dwell most often in the realm of the mind. Shifting fully into the leader mindset is incredibly challenging for those who have spent years as successful individual contributors. It's also challenging for experienced leaders who struggle to let go of the strategies and skills that brought them into leadership.

The leader mindset contains what I like to call the three leadership superpowers: self-awareness, presence and resilience. They're all important, and they're all learnable skills.

The coach's job is to help the client remove roadblocks standing in the way of the leader mindset. These can be new or longstanding, self-imposed or external. From mindset shift to behavior change, from behavior change to habit formation, from habit formation back to mindset shift. This is the leader's journey.

The first collection of analogies is all about what's going on in the mind of the leader.

1

⤙

Your leadership
super suit

If you've had a kid or a sibling in the past 20 years, you've probably come across *The Incredibles*. Pixar made a big, loud, hilarious farce of superhero movies that cuts across generations and is worth watching multiple times.

But my favorite part of the film (and its sequel) isn't a character or a scene. It's the super suit.

Each superhero gets their own. It has to accommodate their size, their shape and their unique gifts. If you stretch almost limitlessly, the suit stretches too. If you can produce fire, the suit keeps you cool. If you're strong enough to lift a car, the suit keeps up with the way you move.

A superhero would never save the world by wearing something they bought off the rack. Yet how many of us feel like the role we occupy at work is ill-fitting, uncomfortable or inauthentic?

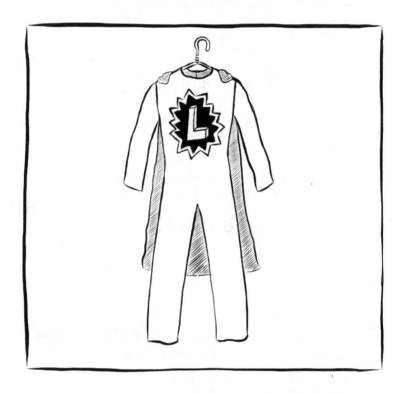

I once worked for two leaders in a row who had exactly the same role. One wore a utility work uniform to the office every day, the other an immaculately-tailored suit. What they wore was a product of their vast differences in identity, culture, background and style.

I think of the persona, or outward-facing identity, as the leadership super suit. It's custom-built. No two are alike. You can wake up in the morning without it on, feeling like yourself. Then you put it on and still feel like yourself, or even more so.

4

Your super suit must play to your strengths and feel comfortable and authentic. If it doesn't, everyone around you will know the difference.

COACHING PROMPTS:

- Do you feel more or less like yourself when you're showing up as a leader? Why?
- What authentic characteristics make up your leadership persona?

2

~~⌒⌒~~

Secure your own mask
before helping others

This is probably among the best-known analogies since the dawn of aviation. And we won't even get into the politics of mask-wearing that have sprung up in the United States during pandemic times. But still, it's as simple and true as the act of leadership itself. You must look after your own needs before you can look after the needs of others.

On a plane, you're advised to secure your own oxygen mask first. This goes against parental instinct, filial piety and just plain neighborliness, but it makes sense. If you pass out in a depressurized plane cabin, you're not going to be able to help anyone who can't put their mask on by themselves.

Some of the world's most effective leaders blend humility and selflessness with a desire to excel and be recognized. But this effectiveness is not sustainable over time without self-care. You can also call it self-resourcing, or protecting

the asset. Done properly, it is the foundation upon which leadership is built. If you don't mind your physical and mental health, take breaks and find balance in your life, no one else will do it for you. In the long run, this is a recipe for diminished performance, stress and burnout.

I've grappled with self-care and have coached dozens of leaders through paying more attention to it. It's important for every human being, but it's essential for those who lead others. Remember that your team is watching your example. Show them how it's done.

COACHING PROMPTS:

- Which parts of your well-being do you wish you could give more attention? What would be necessary for you to do that?
- In what ways can you demonstrate your leadership by taking better care of yourself?

Coaching prompts:

- Where can you see yourself needing more flexibility in your planning and delegation with your team? Needing less flexibility?
- How might some more transparency help you avoid unpleasant surprises?

4

Seeing beyond the hood ornament

I'm old enough to remember when most cars had hood ornaments. Not way back when they used to be the cap for a radiator, but when they were the expression of prestige for an automotive brand. Mercedes had the three-pointed star in a circle. People used to try to steal them.

Aerodynamics and collision safety pretty much finished off hood ornaments decades ago. But they're still adorning the Rolls-Royce, and they're still a useful way to think about perspective.

If you're not looking past the end of the hood when you drive, you're missing upcoming exit signs and interesting scenery. You could also miss the distracted driver in the next lane or the taillights of an 18-wheeler up ahead that is about to stop suddenly.

At work, we expect our employees to keep their heads down and focus on their work. But we need our leaders to do more. Leaders must look up, down and sideways, and bring the benefit of their perspective to their teams. If they don't, they will miss many threats and opportunities.

COACHING PROMPTS:

- When do you tend to keep your head down, instead of taking a more global perspective?
- What can you do to allow yourself more time and space to look at your work more broadly?

5

~~🙡~~

At 40,000 feet,
or stooping to
pick up a dime?

"He's totally unpredictable. Sometimes I can't get his attention when I need it, and sometimes I've got all of his attention when I need none of it. I can never tell if he's going to stay at 40,000 feet or stoop to pick up a dime." — Actual quote by the author, to a coworker in a past job.

The CEO who likes to pitch in during tough times and support the boots on the ground? That's inspiring. The CEO who likes to line-edit press releases when there are four layers of staff between him and the person who writes them? That's a problem.

Few things will demotivate a good employee faster than having their boss parachute in, express a snap opinion and override a decision that should have been the employee's call.

It undermines expertise and hard work, and it completely blurs lines of authority. Of course the boss can make the final decision on anything — that's why they're the boss. But that doesn't mean they should.

If a leader shows this pattern of behavior over time, it can leave their team second-guessing their roles or even their competence. It can also lead to undermining. If someone else in the organization doesn't like the decision you've made, they can just go to the boss and get it overruled.

As a leader-turned-coach, my general belief is that actions and decisions belong as low on the org chart as possible. This is part of the recipe for the best use of resources and for growth. But consistency is the other part of that recipe.

If you have established lines of authority in your organization, stick to them. If special circumstances warrant more involvement than usual, explain them. Let your people do their jobs, and you'll let them know they've earned your trust.

COACHING PROMPTS:

- How clear are the lines of authority in your organization? Do members of your team know when you want to be involved and when you don't?
- What can you do to empower your team with more decision-making ability?

6

~~⊃

Make sure you have the votes

We introverts don't love surprises. Being put on the spot in a meeting is a joy for verbal processors, but for those who are a bit more reserved or need time to think things through, it can lead to disaster. It can make coming to a meeting feel like being unprepared for combat, even if you're the one leading the meeting.

I had a client who was struggling with some of these dynamics when I brought in an analogy from my past work life. In legislative politics, you don't want an antagonistic lawmaker to consign your bill to the dust heap or amend it beyond recognition. You want to know it will pass before you put it on the floor for a vote. Or, if you're trying to kill a bill and don't want your fingerprints on it, you bring it up for a vote when you know it will fail.

The same can be true for any company meeting that you're driving toward a known outcome. Find out who your

supporters are, and who you need to spend more time with to win their support. Who has the ultimate veto power? Who will have a speaking role, and who will signal their assent from the sidelines? How important is visibility for you here? Does it make sense for you to be the standard-bearer, or should someone else with more stature or credibility take the lead? If the outcome you're seeking is to keep a bad idea from rising into fruition, the process is the same.

This is harder work in a virtual environment, of course. You won't be able to simply commandeer a conference room a few minutes early with a key player or two. It makes intentional, offline conversations even more important. Putting more time and space around preparation is something to consider.

COACHING PROMPTS:

- What is my desired outcome, and how can I make sure I get it before the meeting?
- Who are my key stakeholders who can help accomplish my outcome? What will these stakeholders need to be comfortable speaking up for what we all want?

7

The talented locksmith

One day, you come back from your morning run to discover you've locked your keys in your house. Assuming you don't have a landlord nearby, or a lockbox or a neighbor with a spare key, you're going to need some professional help. It's time to call a locksmith.

Even leaving aside anything that could make this situation worse — it's raining, you have to pee, the dog is inside and also has to pee — time is not really on your side here. You need someone who can show up and get the job done fast.

Experience matters. You're not going to feel great about paying a locksmith at all because you made a mistake. But wouldn't it feel better to pay someone who can turn the tumblers and open the door in a matter of a few seconds than someone who would take an hour or two to do the same job? Wouldn't you think the faster fix is the better deal?

And yet, doesn't it seem like the world of full-time, salaried knowledge work values the two-hour locksmith instead of the 60-second one? I spend a lot of time talking to clients about time and attention management, and the expectations that the working world places on how they do both.

Stop me if any of these seems familiar:

- I'll get on top of my workload if I just work some more hours.

- The more I work, the more I'll advance the mission of my employer — saving animals, providing clean water, making it possible for kids to go to school.
- Working harder, or more, sets me apart from my colleagues.

One man's opinion here, formed over a number of years: the "butts in seats" model is a lousy way to measure employee effectiveness.

This lesson first hit me many years ago. The head of the organization where I worked seemed bothered by the fact that I was leaving at 5:30 every day — the end of the business day, per the employee handbook. I was meeting my milestones and getting good reviews. The organizational culture still continued to value extra hours and probably still does today.

We've now had more than a year of a pandemic to teach us that for many jobs, success doesn't rely on spending 8+ hours a day, 5+ days a week in a physical office anymore. In some parts of our economy, flexible hours and telework are now part of the draw away from organizations that are sticking with the old model. So we can add turnover risk to burnout and disengagement.

You can be an effective employee and still take your kid to the orthodontist, or get your washing machine fixed or take some time to be in your thoughts. In fact, doing these things will probably make you a more effective employee.

We're human beings, not units of production. Working more doesn't mean working better. As leaders, it's on us to model this attitude for the people who look up to us — and to hire people who are more like expert locksmiths than technicians on a time clock.

Coaching prompts:

- When was the last time you took an actual day off? As in, you didn't do any work or check in with work?
- Which areas of your non-work life, if you paid them more attention, would actually make you a more effective employee or leader?

P.S. Having a lockbox with a key in it is a very handy thing. You can stash it somewhere out of the way, and use it if a guest, house-sitter or contractor needs to get in — or if you do.

8

~⌒つ

Waiting for the fire alarm

Knowledge workers often confuse "busy" with "effective." When the modern workplace puts a premium on activity, the modern employee feels compelled to respond. Who among us hasn't generated *work product* — a flurry of slides, documents, emails — to justify taking up a salary or a desk?

During the pandemic, this workism or performative busyness popped up in organizations where the boss was uncomfortable with telework. If I can't see them, how will I know they're working? How will I know we're getting our money's worth?

Downtime is a reality, and a need for all of us. Some people are more efficient than others in their work (see the previous analogy about the locksmith for one example). Not all jobs are supposed to take 40+ hours a week of our time.

What if we could take a tiny bit of inspiration from a group of people we happily pay to spend much of their time *not* doing the thing that is their primary job?

Firefighters.

They're at that fire station for long shifts, sometimes days at a time. They're keeping themselves in good physical shape. Maintaining equipment. Attending training. Catching up on their reading and watching. Perfecting their chili recipes. And waxing every ambulance and fire engine into luminescence. As soon as that alarm rings out, they're down the pole and out the door.

We pay firefighters to save lives and property. But we also pay them to be available to save lives and property when it's needed.

It's not efficient at all from a staffing perspective. You can't run a fire station like you run a Starbucks. And paying firefighters like freelancers, for every call they handle, wouldn't make sense at all. The available capacity is an important part of the bargain they strike.

I've recently begun taking more of a firefighter approach to my own work as well.

I *hate* charging for missed coaching sessions, because I want my clients to get the maximum value out of our engagements. At the same time, I've learned to accept that my clients also pay me to be available for them. A no-show or a last-minute cancellation means I can't be available for somebody else during that time. So I have become more comfortable with the idea of being here, helmet in hand, ready to slide down that pole if the alarm rings.

COACHING PROMPTS:

- Are you paying your employees only to work, or also to be available for work?
- If the former, to what extent do you have a culture of busyness around you?

9

⮌

Running past a bicycle

I always ask my clients how they've been doing since the last time we spoke. I've lost track of the number of times "busy" was the answer. We're hooked on busyness as a work culture in the United States. We measure ourselves and others by it too.

It's essential for leaders to pull their heads out of "busy" to be effective. It's also very, very difficult.

Let's say you need to go somewhere, and you've decided the best way is to run there. You lace up your shoes and put one foot in front of the other. You're off. You run, and run, and run.

At some point, your legs, your lungs, your arms are starting to scream at you that they're tired. You try not to notice. You are so entirely focused on the act of running to your destination that you've tuned out your surroundings. And so, you completely miss a very important piece of information.

A half mile ago, you passed a shiny hybrid bicycle with a FREE sign on it. It has plenty of air in the tires, and a helmet hanging off the handlebars that's perfectly sized for your head. All of this escaped your notice.

Catching that bicycle would require you to do two things: slow down enough to see it and realize it can help you, and actually stop running to climb aboard. If you did, you'd have a new and better way to get where you're going with less effort.

I wouldn't suggest doing this during a race. Crossing the finish line of a running race on a bicycle is a great way to get disqualified and irritate your fellow runners. But sometimes you do have to slow down to speed up, or to work smarter.

COACHING PROMPTS:

- How has busyness prevented you from taking a fresh perspective on leadership that might be helpful?
- Can you step back to build a plan, a process or a team that would make your business unit even more effective?

10

~~∂~~

The boulder and the forklift

If every organization simply agreed to every budget request, every organization would be broke. Leaders with budgetary authority constantly make decisions of priority, spreading resources across areas where they feel they can make the most impact.

Yet almost every leader I've spoken to has felt resource constraints at some point. I've felt this myself during my own career. "If we could only get a few extra bodies," the conversation begins. I've coached some of my more reserved clients through the process of advocating for those resources, knowing that the more outspoken leader often wins the day in this kind of quest.

But what if throwing more bodies at the problem isn't the best solution?

I once asked a client to imagine finding just a few more hands to help move a large boulder out of the road so traffic can proceed. At some point, you have too few people to make

11

⤳

Pushing papers, cleaning cages

Nearly every rising leader I've met struggles with the issue of impact. It is easy to measure your impact when you're doing the work. What was your call completion rate? How many widgets did you ship? As a leader, you *do* a lot less than you direct, motivate or inspire.

At best, this is abstract. At worst, it's completely demoralizing.

I know this because I've been there.

I once ran the communications shop for a global animal advocacy nonprofit. This is an issue set that's been close to my heart for decades — I've followed a plant-based diet for 20 years and have had animals at home since I was a small child. The union of my professional skill set and my wish for a more compassionate world seemed like a dream. Until,

predictably, I started coming home at night and wondering *what exactly did I accomplish today?*

I led the team that communicated the stories about the field workers, litigators and policy professionals who were working to make the world better for animals. I was several degrees of attenuation away from the work itself. My job was dozens of meetings every week, expense reports, time sheets and the tiniest bit of writing and editing. Just how much did my own efforts matter? To this day, I have no idea.

I could tell you how many media mentions we had earned, how many likes we got on social media, how many videos we posted or how many pages of magazine we printed. These are important metrics, but they're not direct measures of impact on a mission of change.

I had a near-constant craving for something tangible. CEOs and other executives get to measure their effectiveness through the output of the business units they lead. I was a middle manager. I later learned that many of my colleagues would scratch their tangible itch by volunteering at their local animal shelters on weekends.

So, are you pushing papers or cleaning cages?

COACHING PROMPTS:

- How do you measure the impact of your work, and of the work of those you lead?
- Does this feel sufficiently tangible for you? If not, what are some ways you can work to give yourself a sense of tangible impact?

12

~⊃

Freshly cut grass
on your boots

You've been cutting lawns since you were in high school and needed gas money. There's something you just love about the fresh air and the smell of freshly cut grass on your boots. One day, you look down and realize you haven't actually worn boots in years. Your dress shoes have not a single blade, not a hint of green on them.

You are the successful owner of a chain of landscaping businesses. You're responsible for personnel, equipment, real estate, all manner of things that are necessary for serving customers who want tidy lawns. But you don't cut the grass and you haven't in the longest time. Instead, you lead a team of people who lead teams of people who cut the grass.

The impact of your work is exponentially larger than it was. Your company manages hundreds of landscaping contracts — literally acres upon acres more mowing than

you'd be able to do yourself with a single machine. Still, you miss that smell more than a little.

I have coached many leaders who yearn for the past days of cutting the grass themselves. It might have been easier to leave work behind at the end of the day. The *doing* was simpler, easier to quantify than the *being, directing and enabling* an executive-level position requires.

Sometimes they wish they could cut grass again. And sometimes they actually do so, either intentionally or unintentionally. The trick is to find meaning and fulfillment in that expanded impact, and to grow comfortable with one's own value being expressed through the work of others.

COACHING PROMPTS:

- Are you taking on a task, an assignment or a role because it's the best expression of your abilities and perspective? Or are you doing it because it's comfortable and familiar?
- How might you expand your impact by further enabling your team to do its work?

(Hat tip to the incomparable coach and author Scott Eblin for originating this analogy and giving me permission to use it.)

SECTION 2

~⊃

Communication

I started my career as a television journalist almost 25 years ago. It brought the adrenaline rush of being live on the air, the scramble to hit a deadline, the novelty of being recognized in the grocery store on occasion. These things are long gone, buried somewhere in my psyche.

What never left was the desire to use words and images to advance understanding. To take something specific and complicated and help non-experts understand it. This is what I did for many years after what turned out to be a short stint in broadcasting. I navigated the nonprofit, government and utility sectors first as a communicator and then as a leader of communicators.

To shift from being a comms guy to being a leadership coach would seem to be a rather dramatic pivot. But I think it's more of an evolution than a pivot.

Communication is *everything* in leadership. It affects how others see you and how much impact you have. I'm so pleased to help my clients through their struggles with communication — either in stepping forward more, or in honing their messages to make them more effective.

The following pages come straight from this important work.

1

Don't just have the soup

A nonprofit leader had a direct report who wasn't following her instructions. She couldn't figure this out — was it stubbornness, incompetence, something entirely different? During our coaching session, I was able to help her crack the code. She wasn't expressing herself clearly or forcefully enough to be heard, or perhaps to be taken seriously. Being more direct made her uncomfortable, and correcting the mistake or misperception after the fact made her more uncomfortable.

I asked my client to imagine having a nice dinner out, and making her choice of a complement to the main dish. Let's say it's a hot day and you order a salad, I suggested. A few minutes later, the server comes back from the kitchen with a bowl of piping hot minestrone and offers to grind some fresh pepper on it for you.

Do you remind the server that you asked for a salad? Or, do you think to yourself, "It's fine. Someone took the trouble

to make this soup and pour me a bowl. I don't want to waste it. It's not that important. I'll just have the soup."

My client smiled. "I would totally do that," she said. "And I hate soup!"

When you're the leader, you get to have preferences and express them for others to follow. In fact, you have to do this. If you don't, nobody on your team will have a sense of direction or know how they can grow in their roles. So, how to ease into this after a lifetime of backing away from what might seem like a conflict?

A good server will often replay everyone's order before leaving the table to eliminate any ambiguity and make mistakes less likely. I asked my client what might happen if she suggested her employee read back their understanding of the request before an interaction is over.

The client said this readout would probably help make her instructions more clear. She also pledged to build a practice of reiterating and reminding… instead of just living with the soup.

COACHING PROMPTS:

- Are you making requests, or giving directions, clearly?
- What do you do if you get something that doesn't meet your standards?

2

30-60-90 design

I've had the pleasure of coaching many clients who say they want to speak up more in meetings. They're aiming for some more visibility for their team or business unit. Or their leadership has told them that they have an important perspective — and they need to communicate it more effectively.

As an introvert who has spent many thousands of hours of my life in meetings, I can relate. The first step is to figure out what's holding the leader back from participating. It's a slightly different story for everyone, but I noticed a common ingredient among my highly technically skilled clients who were finding their way into leadership.

Certainty.

Accustomed to working in a world where there is a right answer and a wrong one — say, accounting or engineering — these leaders didn't want to say something and be proven

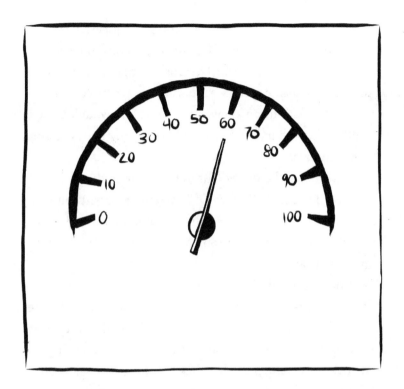

wrong later. Their lack of certainty, or lack of desire to state a tentative opinion, was keeping them quiet.

With one of these clients, I introduced the idea of 30-60-90 percent design, a concept I picked up from my days in municipal government. When you're building an infrastructure project, like a bridge or a big underground pipe, you invite comments and make revisions in stages. The later the stage of the project, the more you move from making wholesale changes into refining. Enough of the stakeholders fall in line to keep the design phase on track.

What if instead of aiming for 100 percent certainty before speaking up, or even 90 percent certainty, the client went for 60 percent instead? Everyone in the room would likely understand that she was sharing her perspective based on the information she knew at the time. She wouldn't need to undermine the information she was sharing by suggesting it was tentative.

And what if she turned out to be wrong in the end? It happens all the time. She would have ample opportunity to express a new opinion, or a slightly modified one, if her colleagues were more accustomed to hearing from her on a regular basis anyway.

What if the working environment placed a different set of expectations on women, people of color or others who are historically underrepresented in leadership — that they were under pressure to be right more often? This is where allies and advocates come into play. Picture a team of engineers presenting the 60 percent bridge design. Who else can help speak up for an idea, or to make sure the presenter's idea is heard in the first place?

COACHING QUESTIONS:

- To what extent does a desire for certainty hold you back from expressing your opinion?
- What is the value your organization places on being right, versus being present and being a participant?

3

~~⌒~~

TIME Magazine and Twitter

W hen I look back on the start of my brief career in television news, I can hardly believe it's been a quarter century since that time. I also remain incredibly grateful *every single day* that I was a broadcaster before the dawn of social media.

True, the need to cultivate a digital persona carries many risks and pitfalls. But I'm more concerned about never-ending deadlines and the pressure to dribble out parts of stories in tweet form. So I'm glad I never had to do that. And yet something similar has come up in coaching.

Among my clients, some of my fellow introverts are reserved and like to get it right. They don't want to risk speaking up in a meeting or taking an opinion on an issue until they've done all of their homework. As a result, they can be seen as too cautious. They can miss their moment to weigh in and influence a decision because others have

stepped into the space. I ask them to consider what would happen if they knew less and spoke sooner.

In other words, are you TIME Magazine, or are you Twitter?

As a news consumer, I find value in both. I'm old enough to love the feel of a well-produced printed magazine in my hands at the end of the week, with the benefit of long-form narrative, curated photojournalism and a wider lens on the events of the world. Yet if something is happening in real time and I'm interested in how it unfolds, it is hard to beat the unfiltered and live quality of social media.

I once had a news director who liked to say, "The best kind of story is a done story." In other words, it doesn't matter how well-reported or accurate the story is if you miss your deadline and it isn't on the air for anyone to hear it.

COACHING PROMPTS:

- How is the need for certainty reducing your opportunities to express yourself — either to be more visible or to make a necessary point?
- What are the true risks of speaking up sooner and potentially getting it wrong?

4

⌒つ

Cook the pantry,
or use a recipe?

I'm an introvert who enjoys speaking in public, so I love when clients come to me with challenges on this front.

I am not a speaking coach. Every major city has at least a handful of talented professionals who can help with breathing exercises, where to place your hands and the other more physical aspects of speaking when you're already on stage. My realm is what's going on in the mind beforehand.

I help clients get themselves into the right headspace to present effectively. But even before that moment, I help them discover what kind of advance work they need to do.

Just as we have different styles in speech, we have different styles in preparation. I think it's just as possible to over-prepare as it is to under-prepare.

Are you the sort of cook who needs to follow a recipe to the teaspoon? Or do you enjoy knowing you have a

good assortment of ingredients you can round up to invent something new?

If your dinner requires you to include a full day's supply of Vitamin C, you're likely going to disappoint your nutritionist if you end up going the improv route. But stick really closely to a recipe for comfort, and watch what happens in your head when you realize you're missing an ingredient.

When you prepare to speak in public, do you give yourself a collection of key points and build on them as you're talking, knowing you will likely miss a few details

— but your audience is highly unlikely to notice? Or, do you read from your script, having full confidence that everything you need to say is laid out in front of you? The risk is less connection with your audience, and possibly the inability to get back if you lose your place.

COACHING PROMPTS:

- What is the least amount of written material you'd be comfortable taking into a speaking engagement? Why?
- Are you more concerned with delivering essential details, or leaving a general impression on a topic?

5

⟿

New glasses, or new nose?

Coaching is the best way I know of to bring about transformation in leaders. Some clients end their engagements with subtle shifts in energy and behavior. Others have huge breakthroughs and end up taking their work lives in an entirely different direction. The coach is the same guy, so the size and speed of change is up to the client. I've found it's helpful to ask what they want early on.

A client in financial technology was seeking change in how others perceived him. He was thoughtful and even-tempered, and he had a solid reputation in the company. Still, he felt almost invisible at times. Colleagues weren't including him in cross-functional discussions as often as he wanted. He didn't want to spend his entire time there boxed into a single role.

In our first session, I asked him how big of a change he wanted his colleagues to notice if we were successful together. Was it a scale of change along the lines of getting new glasses — you see things more clearly, your face is

outlined in a slightly different way, and it's subtle enough for some people to miss? Or was it a scale of change along the lines of getting a new nose — your entire facial identity is different, and it cannot be ignored?

Turns out this client wasn't looking for a new nose. He was seeking to add onto his existing presence more gradually, to the point that colleagues might notice the end result but not the work in progress. We decided to work together on thoughtful self-expression as a first step.

CoACHING PROMPTS:

- What is the scale of change you are hoping to achieve? How soon?
- What does too much change, too fast, look like for you?

6

The hole in the wall

"Sell the hole, not the drill." It's one of the only things I remember from advertising class my freshman year of college — other than settling into my dorm room to watch a recording of the Super Bowl and fast-forwarding through the game to watch the commercials.

It's a quote attributed to Leo McGivena, an advertising executive who died more than 40 years ago. The idea is beloved in businesses that promote a sharing economy, despised among those who are loyal to certain brands of power tools. To me, as someone who never worked in advertising, sales or home improvement, the resonance is simple.

Your solution is never, *ever* going to be as important to your audience as the problem they were trying to solve in the first place. The presenting problem is the focus, and the finer points of your solution are just details.

It doesn't matter how innovative or elegant your solution is. It doesn't matter how long it took you to devise, or how brilliant you were in devising it. And it doesn't matter who your audience is either. Your boss, your team, your board of directors or your business partner brought you a problem. The conversation in which you introduce your solution must center on the problem first, and move as quickly as possible to the outcome. Process matters much, much less. So does detail.

First, you must consider time and attention. Assume that your stakeholder has multiple problems in need of solution at the same time. Perhaps they need a hole in the wall *and* the ice maker stopped working *and* someone needs to watch the kids tonight. Their bandwidth for thinking about your solution is limited.

Second, think about expertise. If your stakeholder were the expert on how to solve their own problem, you wouldn't be having this conversation. You figured it out. Assuming you have the relationship and the credibility to back up the solution, the technical details of how you arrived here are less important.

Start with the problem, bridge to the outcome. That's how they'll count on you to deliver the right hole.

Coaching prompts:

- When reporting on your progress or a conclusion, how can you take out a few process details to make the conclusion clearer?
- What is the minimum level of detail necessary for your stakeholder to trust your conclusion?

7

⌒꙳

Structural integrity, or coat of paint?

Many a client struggles with giving critical feedback to members of their team. It's uncomfortable. It seems confrontational. It may not work properly. All of this makes a juicy topic for a coaching conversation.

And yet, many leaders miss a key part of the "how" of feedback as they struggle with the "what."

The missing piece is how you set up the meeting. You must *not*, under any circumstances, send a calendar invite to your direct report without any information in it. Nor may you allow your assistant to do so. Especially if the meeting happens to fall late in the afternoon and late in the week in your employee's time zone.

This is because we all make up stories in the absence of information. If your relationship with your direct report

isn't open and strong, or if you don't interact all that often, a blank meeting invite is unnecessarily terrifying. Nothing like sweating through your shirt as you sit in the comfy chairs outside your boss's office. I know because I've been there.

If you're setting a meeting with a direct report to deliver feedback, offer at least some guidance on the type of feedback and how serious it is.

Are you talking about the structural integrity of the building being at risk, or are you asking for a new coat of paint? And, will the two of you be talking about ways to shore up the building together, or looking at paint swatches?

Give your internal processors some time to reflect on what might be coming and how to process it. Surprises and feedback don't mix.

COACHING PROMPTS:

- Before delivering critical feedback, how can you best prepare your staffer to be open to receiving it and responding to it?
- What is possible if the person absorbs the feedback along with your intent in giving it? What is at risk if the person does not do so?

8

⟿

The donut and the hole

"We're always so focused on the donut around here," a boss and mentor once told me, "So I'm glad you are good at focusing on the hole."

She was thanking me for making observations that led to process improvements at a fast-growing startup. (And not calling me a complainer, I hope.) But this also got me thinking about my relationship to positive versus constructive feedback.

As leaders, we must make sure our reports know where they stand with us. Humans are masterful at inventing stories to fill in gaps in information. We don't want them to bring these stories into their relationships with us.

I've worked in plenty of environments where the only kind of input was rare and critical. If you didn't hear anything from management, you could assume you were doing your job well. Get summoned upstairs and it's a bad

day. My experience is that it's hard to grow and thrive in a leadership culture like this one. Some leaders say they don't have the time to spend on giving feedback to their staff. I'd argue they should make the time.

Positive feedback is important for growth and development. It can be hard to deliver sometimes, especially for a leader who isn't accustomed to receiving it. It's a skill that takes practice on both sides.

There's an irony to this whole donut business for me. Many of my fellow vegans go absolutely wild over donuts. I live with two of them. Not me. The only part of the donut

I can eat without feeling slightly nauseous afterwards is the hole.

COACHING PROMPTS:

- What can you do to blend more positive feedback into your performance critiques?
- What is your level of comfort in providing compliments?

9

The floor mats

You don't coach the person who's not in the room. Speculating about the motivations of a client's supporting cast, or the meaning behind their actions, can be a distraction. Coaching is about behavior change for the client, not for the people around them.

Still, many of my clients want to talk through the process of giving feedback to their direct reports.

One client had someone who was young, ambitious and successful on his team. Let's call this person Manny. He showed up as many things my client did not — outwardly confident and talkative, to name a couple. And the client now needed to guide Manny into dialing back some of those very qualities that had made him successful at the company.

The executives are talking about this guy, he told me. He's got their attention. But he doesn't know when to *stop*. "It's like selling them the floor mats when they've already bought the car."

The client went on to explain that Manny's reputation was at risk because influential leaders at the company could start to tune him out in meetings. If he takes the argument too far, he loses the room.

For starters, I wondered whether Manny was even aware of this tendency he had developed. If so, my client could go straight to developing solutions. If not, he'd have to work to raise that awareness. If he and Manny were in the same meeting, could he flash some kind of a signal that it was time to wrap up the conversation? Stage managers and conference organizers do this sort of thing all the time, after all.

In my mind, I saw my client holding up a picture of a floor mat.

COACHING PROMPTS:

- What are the signs — verbal and nonverbal — that you've won your audience over to your point of view?
- What might be a danger or a missed opportunity that arises from continuing to advocate past the point of winning?

10

The slumber party parent

A group of coaches were on a Zoom call, talking about something we'd seen over and over again in our clients and in our own work. No matter how kind, open and collaborative a leader is, the leader's presence in the room has an impact on the meeting.

The leader might cause a chilling effect, if someone feels less free to speak up fully with an authority figure present. The leader might drive an outcome, even unintentionally, by making a suggestion in the midst of brainstorming or offering an opinion early in the meeting. Or the leader might take the conversation in a certain direction by asking questions to learn more.

Simply put, you can't be the most senior person in a meeting and not have it be your meeting. Or, as one of my colleagues put it, "It's like your mom showing up at a slumber party."

We must resist a tumble down the slippery slope of all the ways we could compare leadership to parenting. Still, this one's a nice fit.

If you're mom, you can pay for pizza, make sure the movie is appropriate for the audience and check on the number of pillows. But the moment you plop yourself down in the middle of the group with a bowl of popcorn and a "Whazzzup?" is the moment the conversation stops. Your role is to make everyone feel welcome, keep half an eye on the liquor cabinet and stay out of the way.

In meetings, you might consider speaking last after everyone has been heard. You could work the whiteboard instead of sitting at the head of the table. And you can certainly amplify voices by calling on the more reserved folks in the room.

Or you could simply choose not to go at all.

COACHING PROMPTS:

- How can you provide your staff with the opportunity to explore their ideas together without having an impact on that exploration yourself?
- What are three meetings in the next week that you can opt out of attending?

(Hat tip to Eric Couillard for the inspiration for this analogy.)

11

The misdirected airplane

Setting direction and communicating that direction are among the leader's most important responsibilities. As is the well-timed check-in to make sure the team is still on course. With too many touch points, you're micromanaging. With too few, you're setting yourself up for late surprises.

You are not providing turn-by-turn directions. You're setting the course and making sure everyone stays on it.

Imagine two planes taking off at the same time on parallel runways, bound for the same destination. To the untrained eye, they're both aimed in exactly the same direction. But one of them is aimed just 10 degrees north of the other.

If both planes stick to their respective courses for the three hours they're in the air, only one of them will reach its intended destination on time. The other will be hundreds of miles away, over a different city or even a different time zone.

Of course, a modern jetliner's sophisticated navigation system would prevent this scenario from happening. An experienced pilot with a map and a pencil would work as a backup. But the different city, different time zone scenario happens too often in work.

A member of the team starts out feeling like they're headed to the right place and pointed in the right direction. Weeks if not months later, the boss says, "No, this isn't what I had in mind at all." Both sides are frustrated and wondering about the other's ability to carry out their respective jobs. And the situation was completely preventable.

Make sure your planes are aimed at the right destination. Verify periodically that they remain on course.

COACHING QUESTIONS:

- What is your process for getting your staff aligned at the beginning of a new initiative?
- How do you provide them the autonomy and flexibility to carry out the work, while staying informed enough to know if they start tracking off course?

SECTION 3

⤳

Time and Attention

Try to be everywhere and do everything, or to be all things to all people, and you'll quickly run into your limits. I like to say that the leader's time and attention are their most precious resources. It's incredibly easy to allow these to be misdirected and over-committed by the competing demands of the work.

Feeling like you're so caught up in responding to the demands of others that you don't have time and space for your own work? Showing up in a meeting only to wonder why you're there and how it got on your calendar? These are symptoms that your time and attention are out of balance. The good news is that this situation is well within your control.

With time, your team will help you preserve your time and attention for the things you must do that they cannot. The analogies in this chapter have helped my clients understand where they are and where they need to be.

1

Sand, pebbles and rocks

One theme has come up in almost every coaching engagement I've had: the leader's time and attention are their most important resources. Safeguarding these resources is some of the most important foundational work a leader can do. It's also never been harder.

Say yes to everyone, or allow yourself to be pulled away by every distraction, and you've got nothing left for your own objectives. Become a professional hermit and devote yourself to Cal Newport's *Deep Work*, and you're missing the important human elements of the role.

Think about a table in front of you, with a large mason jar, a pile of big rocks, a pile of pebbles and a pile of sand next to it. All of these things were once in the jar, and it's your job to put them back.

The order matters.

If you start with the sand, you'll end up with no room for the big rocks. Same for starting with the pebbles. You

have to put the big rocks back in the jar first, followed by the pebbles, followed by the sand. The smaller elements fit around the bigger ones.

Think about how this goes in the world of work. Do you ever open a browser to do something specific, only to find yourself scrolling Twitter or Instagram a half hour later? Think of how hard it is to get back on track afterwards. This is what happens when you let sand into your jar first.

Same thing for the leader who can't seem to get any work done because their calendar is booked with meetings with other people all day long. You could simply log back in for a couple hours at night after the kids go to bed, but that's like letting your work day spill past the top of the jar! Instead, I talk to leaders about blocking out time for their important priorities first, and letting others take time slots for meetings after. The big rocks go in first.

Longer days and less time off will be a temporary fix. This isn't a sustainable approach in the long term — in fact, it's a recipe for burnout. You have to protect your time and attention by using them more wisely.

Make room for your big rocks.

COACHING PROMPTS:

- Which big rocks have you had trouble making room for in the jar of your time and attention?
- Could you use a little less sand in your life? What would that look like?

(Note: This analogy was made popular by Stephen Covey in two of his best-selling books. Its origin is unknown.)

2

~~⚬

The 50-pound weight
on your back

In the spring of 2020, I had a client who lamented the mess her organized life had become. She was suddenly juggling being the primary caregiver to two very young kids with her usual full-time work duties — now done from home — and trying to hold herself to pre-pandemic standards of productivity and responsiveness. The inner critic was driving her toward burnout.

American working moms — especially women of color — worked longer hours, faced more burnout and had steeper career setbacks during the early pandemic months than they did in the before times. The working world in general seemed even less oriented toward parents of young children.

The solutions are institutional and societal, but the burden is individual. My first step was to make sure my client knew *she* wasn't the problem here. She couldn't simply outwork it.

So I told her that her situation is like trying to run a race with a 50-pound weight on your back, and then wondering why you're so much slower than the other runners. I know this because I've literally done it.

Some years ago, my wife and I were signed up to run a fall 10K in DC. I'd done this race before and loved the flat course along the Potomac at Hains Point. Our babysitter became ill at the last moment, and most of the friends we would have asked were going to be in the race. So we brought our 5-year-old daughter along, and she joined us for the 6.2 miles. *On my shoulders.*

She disembarked to cross the finish line on her own two feet, but the rest of the time I was running for two. I finished that race 1,444th of 1,476 runners, probably 4 minutes a mile slower than my usual pace. My back and shoulders were sore for a couple of days, and we got a story for the ages. The next few races felt more like sprints because I was 25 percent lighter!

My client emerged from our conversation wanting to give herself a little more grace and a little more space around what she was handling at the time. We had no idea how long this would last, of course.

Caring for family members, navigating hiring freezes or layoffs, onboarding remotely, pushing through Zoom fatigue, returning to the office... these are all extra weights we've been carrying around. Maybe the burden feels almost normal or isn't noticeable after many months. It's still there, though.

If you can grind out another mile or two, you won't always have that weight on your back. You might be wearing different clothes and running on a different course. You might not be as fast as you were before you ran with the weight. Still, when you find yourself running without it, you'll feel so much lighter, faster, even liberated.

Coaching prompts:

- What extra burdens are members of your team carrying at the moment?
- How can you help them feel seen, heard and supported?

3

A toothpaste decision

I had a client who was vacillating on a new piece of furniture for her home office. So many options. So many colors. And it was her first time working from home, so she wanted to make sure she got it right. And the desire to get it right is what kept her from making the decision at all. Many weeks of seeking to avoid buying the wrong desk had kept her from having any desk.

I asked her if she'd ever felt overwhelmed while looking at the toothpaste section in the grocery store. Of course, she had. Flavors, fluoride, gel, whitening... many of these options compete with each other but are owned by the same company. In an ideal world, buying toothpaste wouldn't be so freaking complicated. And yet, it doesn't really matter.

If you make the wrong choice, you're out 3-6 bucks and you get to try again.

Compare this to buying a house. You're looking at floor plans, neighborhoods, walkability, schools, commute times,

taxes — literally dozens upon dozens of factors. It's also the most important financial decision many families will ever make.

If you make the wrong choice, you've got hundreds of thousands of dollars on the line. Not to mention every quality-of-life factor you can imagine.

We are confronted with an unprecedented amount of information on every decision, regardless of the scale or potential consequences. Maybe this means we are making more thoughtful decisions. Or maybe, as in the case of my client, it's all a recipe for analysis paralysis.

The solution is to break the overthinking cycle with a reframing. When my client realized she needed to get off the fence on the desk purchase, she went with the best option based on her view at the time. She decided to let go of the notion that an even better desk might come along in a few weeks and make her second-guess her decision.

As of this writing, she's been enjoying that desk for almost two years now.

COACHING PROMPTS:

- What is the scale of the decision you're about to make?
- What are the known and potential consequences of that decision?

4

~~~

Presidential laundry

An elementary school student's sense of fairness can be legendary. So it was that I had a fun conversation with my daughter a few years ago. She was just at the age where she was starting to be helpful around the house — instead of needing to be distracted or entertained while her mom and I did all of the chores. There's always a lot to do, from making the bed to feeding the dog to doing the dishes. And laundry.

My daughter was outraged, OUTRAGED, when I happened to mention that the President of the United States doesn't do his own laundry.

That's not fair! Why is it that I, as an 8-year-old, must help sort, fold and put away while the most powerful person IN THE WORLD doesn't have to do so?

I explained that the presidency is also likely the most complicated, most impactful job in the world. Having a staffer do the President's laundry helps free up the

President's mind, and schedule, to do the job better. And the person doing the laundry instead of the President is performing an act of national service.

I think she got the idea. In the years since, I've asked a number of clients to consider when they might be unnecessarily doing their own laundry at work. You have a strong and capable staff. You trust them. You depend on them. When was the last time you took a look at your routine, necessary tasks and figured out what you could delegate more? It may feel like a privileged offloading of work, or even like a shirking of responsibilities if you're a doer by nature. But it frees you up to do the things that only you can do as the leader.

My daughter has yet to come back to me with the suggestion that she needs to preserve her energies for homework, or some extracurricular activity, and should therefore be able to staff out her laundry. I suppose it's only a matter of time.

COACHING PROMPTS:

- Is this task, project, meeting or conversation the highest and best use of your time and attention?
- How can you help others understand that your time and attention are your most valuable resources and should be treated that way?

5

Mail the gas bill

Delegation comes up often in my coaching sessions, especially with emerging leaders. They're curious: how can I get my team to perform more effectively on the programs and projects I delegate to them? And I hear a different question in this question: how can I bring myself to fully hand off something I know I can do better?

I ask my clients to think of delegation like mailing the gas bill.

A generation ago, you'd get your gas bill in the mail once a month. You'd sit down with a pen and a check register, write a check, tear the stub off the bill, stuff it all in the envelope with a stamp on it... and deposit it in the nearest mailbox. Digital billing and banking have cut out a lot of the steps for many of us, but I like this example because of the physical finality of the act. When the door slams shut, you're out.

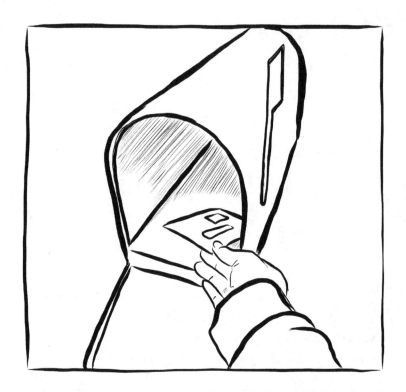

You've exhausted your responsibility by mailing the check. From this point through the gas company crediting your account for the payment, there is *nothing* for you to do. A dozen more things might need to happen next, but they're all in the hands of others. The next time you're supposed to think about the gas bill isn't until next month, when you see the payment on your next bill and have to do it again.

If you really want to, you can call the gas company in a few days to make sure they got your check. But why?

And so it is with a complete, successful delegation. You've given enough input and direction to the person on your team who gets the assignment. You've let them know that the entire process from here until completion is theirs, and you don't need to be involved. You don't need to direct the individual steps that lead them to the outcome. In fact, you don't even need to know what those steps are. They can come to you with an unexpected obstacle or to ask you to clarify your expectations. But the work is theirs. You've handed it off. Completely.

Is this risky? You bet. Is it especially risky if you've spent years of your life doing the exact type of thing you've now asked this team member to do, and building a reputation for being really good at it? Absolutely.

But the doing isn't your job anymore, and neither is being involved in the doing. Your job is to create the space for the other person to do. Perhaps they'll do it less effectively. Perhaps they'll fail. But this is how someone grows into the next person who's known for being really good at that thing. Maybe someday they'll even get better at it than you were.

And if that happens, you'll be a really successful leader for having enabled the growth.

COACHING PROMPTS:

- Are you hanging on to tasks or projects that you could delegate to someone else? Why?
- What would be necessary for you to let go?

6

You're not a bus

"**Y**ou're not a bus. You don't have to let everybody on."

This was unsolicited career advice from a Civil Procedure professor to someone who would eventually become a lawyer client of mine.

The client recalled this little nugget of wisdom some 40 years after she first heard it, when I asked her to tell me her opinion on saying no. She was highly skilled, highly connected and highly paid — and her services were highly in demand as a result. She told me she didn't like to say no, yet she felt like she was working too much.

So it was that she told me about her professor comparing her to public transportation.

Leaders have two resources at their disposal that are more valuable than all the rest: their time and attention. These cannot be swapped out for the time and attention of someone else, and they're expendable — once they're gone,

they're gone. I believe it's incumbent on leaders to protect these valuable resources and for their teams to do the same.

This is why saying no matters. The higher you climb and the longer your career progresses, the more demands you will encounter. Requests for meetings, problem solving, opinion seeking are all things that will take up every last time slot on your calendar and synapse in your brain if you let them.

It feels good to be needed. It feels good to say yes to people who ask for things. Yet taken too far, this principle means you won't have time or energy for your own priorities. Your agenda will be lost if you're constantly in response-to-others mode.

If you've spent any time in a major city, you know the bus isn't the fastest or most comfortable way to get anywhere. Picture a motorcade for that instead. And imagine what would happen if the motorcade stopped every couple of blocks to let people on or off.

Be the motorcade, not the bus.

COACHING PROMPTS:

- What's your relationship with the word "no" at work? Does it depend on who's asking? Why?
- How do you balance wanting to be helpful and collegial with needing to accomplish your own professional goals?

7

~⁀⊃

Life in the batting cage

After a vigorous 19 holes of mini golf, my daughter and I took a break to watch someone in a nearby slow-pitch batting cage. Instead of turning in our putters and tiny pencil, we were entranced.

Pop. Swing. THWACK! Pop. Swing. THWACK!

You need to concentrate and perform, or else you'll miss the ball. Worse, you could get beaned in the head. The timing of your swing is up to you, but the timing of the pitch is up to the machine.

I've never been in an actual batting cage, but I realized something that day. I've had the batting cage feeling plenty of times before, and so have many of the leaders I've coached. It's what happens when you live in your inbox and are constantly captive to the priorities of others.

I think I first got the feeling when I worked in constituent services in city government. It was literally my job to be as responsive as possible. Streetlight? Swing. THWACK! Pothole? Swing. THWACK! It was incredibly

satisfying to solve people's problems in real time. It was also exhausting to think about the fact that there's always, *always* another ball coming your way. The requests never end. I imagine it's similar if you work in a call center or tech support.

In leadership, there's always another ball, too. It's a resource constraint, a personnel issue, an interpersonal dispute on the executive team. Leaders will always have too much to do, and too many people requesting or demanding their attention. This is why they must spend some time, but not too much time, in the batting cage.

The strategy, direction and inspiration only you can provide go missing if you're swinging at every ball that comes your way. Instead, it's time to do some work to figure out what you can delegate, eliminate or ignore.

COACHING PROMPTS:

- How often do you feel like you're in the batting cage at work?
- Can you ignore it, or let someone else handle it, instead of jumping in immediately yourself?

8

⤳

The river or the pool?

In one of my leadership roles, I would average 45-50 meetings a week. Most of them were internal, and they were in my office. It was exhausting for me, and probably even worse for my generally enthusiastic and cheerful assistant who did the scheduling.

These days, my coaching clients complain about their schedules *a lot*. They say they're unable to attend to their own priorities, unable to get out of the weeds, sometimes even unable to get a snack or a cup of coffee because they're tied up in meetings all day.

"Well, am I going to disappoint someone by keeping them waiting, or am I going to use the bathroom for the first time all morning?" one wondered aloud.

I usually press them back on how much or how little control they have over their time. Saying no or sending someone else is an option. Blocking time to be unavailable for meetings is another.

Suppose the schedule is a body of water. When we are navigating our calendar for the week, we're swimming. But bodies of water can be quite different, and we must change the way we are acting around them accordingly.

If your schedule is a river, the current is flowing the way the current flows. You can't stop it or make it change direction by yourself. If you want to swim, you have to be careful. You're looking out for rocks on the banks and rapids in the water. If it's a big and fast river, you're going to go wherever it takes you.

If your schedule is a pool, you've got the water in a finite container built by humans for humans. It's still except for the waves other people are making by diving in. You can sit on the edge and dunk your feet, you can jump in, you can dive. The choice is up to you.

So… river or pool? You may want to figure this out before your next opportunity to take a dip.

COACHING PROMPTS:

- What would your week look like if you eliminated 10 percent of the meetings on your schedule? Which meetings would those be?
- When you block out your own time for deep work or other purposes, what do you do to ensure that others honor the blocks instead of scheduling over them?

9

Free swim

In grade school, I would trundle off to a nearby day camp during the summers. It was an intensely physical experience for a kid who wasn't usually very active. All of those sports and all of those exercises just felt like *work*.

Whether big and athletic or small and nerdy, we all looked forward to free swim. We had a few extra minutes in the pool after our laps. We could float, do some more laps, do handstands, whatever. The choice was up to us, for the only time all day.

I remembered free swim recently when speaking with a client who was struggling with a rogue engineer. The guy was brilliant, but he would dive into research rabbit holes and miss deadlines on key assignments. My client wanted to nurture and reward the creative spirit, while delivering what the company required of his team. He came up with an idea: let his engineer tinker and research freely — potentially coming up with new and innovative projects in the process — *after* the deadline-driven work was complete.

The adult version of free swim, I realized, was Google's 20 Percent Time. The company gives its engineers 20 percent of their business week to explore non-core ideas. Sometimes the extra time leads to interesting discoveries. Sometimes it leads to new products. And sometimes it leads nowhere at all.

Kids and engineers aren't the only ones among us who need to explore. This very book is inspired by the work I do in my coaching practice, but it came about when I gave myself space in my brain to find the words.

COACHING PROMPTS:

- If your schedule had a regular block for non-core work, what might you do with it?
- Who among your staff might benefit from unstructured exploration time? What might the results be for your business?

SECTION 4

~~⌒⊃~~

Relationships

Even if you consider yourself an introvert or somewhat
socially awkward (Hi, I see you!), leadership and
solitude are incompatible. You may have risen to
where you are largely as the result of your own efforts, but
being a leader is a different game. The leader who neglects to
invest in relationships up, down and sideways is neglecting a
critical element of the role.

Relationships are challenging because human beings are
complicated. We have emotions, biases and styles that all
come together in how we interact with the world. Interacting
with us requires holding all of these elements and figuring
out the best way to engage.

At work, relationships rarely stay static even among
people who have known each other for years. A change in
state is a challenge. Many leaders struggle with delivering
critical feedback, or even delivering positive feedback.

In the following pages, you might find a useful reframe for a challenging relationship or interpersonal dynamic in your work life.

1

~~∽~~

Here comes the General

As an introvert who coaches other introverts, I have a lot of conversations with clients about stepping forward. One client had some trouble in this area and realized it was holding her back. She was in a prominent position in the financial sector, with a team who depended on her and younger staff who looked up to her example. She found herself nervous or hesitant when making presentations in front of influential audiences.

I asked her to imagine what it would look like if her parents, partner, mentors, friends and staff were all standing behind her when she was about to have one of these important moments.

She smiled and told me she pictured a Viking army, with her as the general. Complete with spears, shields, battle paint, flags, armor... the whole bit. I said it reminded me of the "here comes the General" moment in *Hamilton*.

Conjuring her mental Viking army has been useful for my client. She now finds herself less nervous and even a little pumped up when she is about to present.

In leadership and in life, you don't need a group that's prepared to do any slaying. The point is that you're not alone. No person's success is solely theirs. All of our work lives are full of people who lifted us up, helped us along or stood by our side at key moments. We carry that support along with us always, no matter what the battle or battlefield.

Coaching prompts:

- When you're facing a moment of stress or uncertainty, whose support can you conjure in your head?
- How might feeling reinforced by your own Viking army help you surmount a challenge?

2

〜

Spinach in my teeth?

I once had a coffee meeting with an old friend I hadn't seen in awhile. I was so glad to have the opportunity to catch up — we had many stories to swap. He looked good, except for one thing.

My friend had a single, solitary hair that had outgrown the bounds of his right nostril and was dangling around in the fresh air. I couldn't bring myself to say a thing! Years later, I still regret this.

This is TOUGH. I've recommended entire, excellent books on the topics of feedback and constructive criticism. I've struggled with it myself. It's about niceness and not disrupting the flow of a relationship.

Often, clients tell me they wouldn't say anything if they discovered a family member was walking around with spinach in their teeth. Then we get to talk about why, and how it's awkward even though having this information would obviously help the other person.

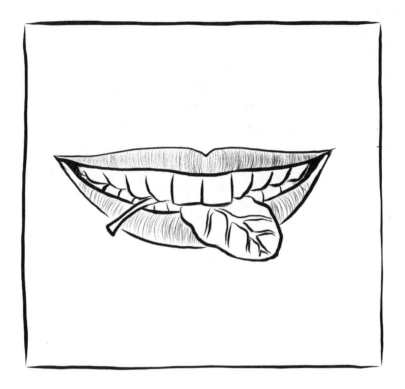

I discovered a related story decades ago when reading an autobiography by broadcasting giant Dan Rather. He was sharing his version of an elevator encounter in a hotel, where the person was looking at him quizzically. Rather thought this was another case of something that would happen to him often: a viewer dumbstruck in the face of celebrity.

Not so, as his fellow passenger finally figured out how to speak up. Turns out Rather's fly was unzipped and a shirt tail was sticking through. He sheepishly said thanks, and wondered how long he had been walking around like that.

Coaching prompts:

- When is constructive or critical feedback actually in service of your relationship with someone?
- If you find yourself holding back on saying something that's on your mind, why?

3

~ ᴐ

Building the better bridge

S ome leaders run headfirst into conflict, while others
avoid it at all costs. I am conflict-averse myself, which
is one of the many reasons I didn't become a litigator
after graduating from law school.

But as a leader and a coach, I've come to realize the value
of constructive conflict.

Not the kind of conflict where your brain feels like
it's at war with the world. Or the kind of conflict where
people tear each other down for sport. I've worked in those
environments too.

Constructive conflict stays in the realm of tasks, not
relationships. It's what happens when people who are good at
their jobs disagree with each other openly, even passionately,
and the outcome improves as a result.

You might find a good example of constructive conflict
in, well... construction.

Imagine a competition to build a new bridge across the river. It's a high-stakes project, with funding from multiple governments and literally thousands of stakeholders. Multiple teams of engineers are vying to come up with possibilities.

If you're one of those engineers, you're ready to go to the mat for your design. It's the absolute best you can imagine in terms of aesthetics, functionality and cost. If your team succeeds, this project will be a career-building highlight for you. You're also up against other extremely talented teams, all of whom also have strong arguments for their bridges.

In the end, only one bridge gets built. The executives have to choose a winner. The other two teams will lose. They got a chance to compete. They'll want the winning team to succeed, of course, and they'll join the entire community in using the new bridge when it's done.

The process, if well-designed and fair, results in a better bridge than if the owner had stuck to a single design from the beginning. At a predetermined point, the conflict ends and the work carries on.

COACHING PROMPTS:

- What role does conflict play in your work as a leader?
- In what ways can you encourage more constructive conflict among members of your team, in service of better results?

4

~ꝵ

The warning light

Something was up, the client said. A colleague who wasn't in his chain of command was underperforming and seemed less engaged than usual. People on my client's team were starting to complain about not getting responses and having to do extra work.

What to do? The client wanted to run through some options. Ignoring the situation wouldn't bring any progress. A direct confrontation wasn't in the cards — the relationship didn't operate on a personal level, and my client wasn't the person's boss. The obvious solution was to go to the supervisor, a colleague of the client.

The tone and substance of the intended conversation were less obvious. My client didn't want to dump a stack of problems on his colleague's desk, potentially provoking some defensiveness. But he did need to see some progress. He seemed stuck on the idea that he didn't know what the actual issue was, and that he wasn't able to find out.

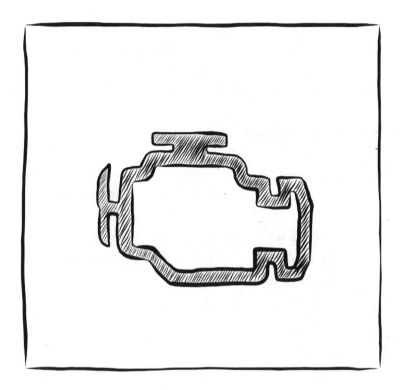

What if he brought along a sense of curiosity instead of
a pointed demand, I wondered. Perhaps his colleague would
appreciate a careful handoff of the situation, with my client
acknowledging the boundaries of his responsibility?

In other words, what if he saw the warning light on the
dashboard and decided to take the car to an expert?

Unless you're a mechanic yourself, the warning light
could mean dozens of different things when it first appears.
You don't know if there is a problem with the light itself —
coming on for no reason — or something seriously amiss
with your engine. You bring it into the shop and describe
what you're seeing and hearing. And then you hand it off.

The mechanic will use your observations if helpful, along with the experience and diagnostic tools that will make the difference in solving the problem. It's your job to notice the alert. The auto expert will do the rest.

COACHING PROMPTS:

- Have you noticed an issue with an employee, a project or a process that you don't know how to resolve?
- What if it's not actually your job to resolve that issue? Who is the right person to approach, and what do they need to know?

5

~⁀⊃

Don't wash the rental car

A client had a challenging relationship with a
member of his team. At the same time, he was
pretty sure this person would soon move to a
different part of the business outside of his span of control.
So it was a sticky situation, but likely a temporary one. The
client was trying to figure out how much effort to put into
patching this relationship and improving the employee's
performance, versus ignoring it until a new supervisor took
over.

I suggested thinking about a rental car. It's the ultimate
in time-limited situations. You're entrusted with the care and
operation of this very valuable thing. You might be driving
members of your family around in it, so you're also entrusting
their safety to the vehicle. It's important for everyone to do
their part in this universe. If you decide to ignore the signs
and light up a smoke while you're driving, the decision comes

with consequences. You're not supposed to go all Blues Brothers on a river crossing either.

And yet, it's not your car. During the time you have it, you don't change the oil, check the fluids or wash it. That's someone else's responsibility, because this is a temporary arrangement. You hand over the keys, and you're done.

My client knew he would continue to do all of the things responsible supervisors do — regardless of how long it took for his staffer's transfer to another department. He also decided that this was likely a matter of months, not years. So he would keep the interactions as light and as pleasant as possible while not investing a ton of time and energy into the future of the relationship. He was, after all, about to hand over the keys to that relationship to someone else.

CoACHING PROMPTS:

- What can you do to show up as an authentic, courageous, thoughtful leader in relationships that could last 5 minutes or many years?
- Which of your relationships might be worthy of more investment? Of less investment?

6

The uncomfortable sofa

We can only coach the person in front of us. And yet, I tend to take note when a client has a recurring character during several sessions. Not long ago, one of my clients kept coming back to the idea that a member of his team was the wrong fit for their job.

Managing up, down and sideways is one of the biggest challenges of being a leader. It can be messy. So, my client continued to ruminate on the impacts of this person not meeting performance expectations. It was as though he was seeking reassurance that his assertion was on track. Or, seeking comfort that any decision about the employee's future would be the right one.

Of course, I can't do these things as a coach. I'd never met the person in question, and we don't substitute our own judgments for those of our clients. What I could do instead is reframe.

Let's say you bought a new sofa, I said. You did the research, read the reviews, swatched the color. Waited for it to arrive, maybe even put it together yourself. And then, after weeks of decision making and anticipation, the moment arrived. You sat down on your new couch.

And it was uncomfortable.

Maybe it'll take some time to break in, you thought to yourself. To soften up those new, stiff cushions. So you wait a few weeks and it feels the same. You think about all of the time, energy and money you put into this purchase. Maybe you even start thinking about what it would take to remove this heavy piece of furniture from your house and find it a new home, and get yourself into a new, more comfortable sofa. It's going to be expensive and it reeks of effort.

So you put the thought out of your mind. You buy some new throw pillows and a fuzzy blanket. And so, after a few more weeks, you have a well-accessorized and still uncomfortable sofa.

The sunk-cost fallacy, the thinking about what it took to get you to this point, is what keeps you from acknowledging that you made a mistake. You simply picked the wrong piece of furniture.

I wondered aloud to my client whether he'd done the same thing with his employee. All of the time spent waiting for a requisition from finance, a job description from HR… all the sifting of resumes, interviews, the onboarding. Vacancies are incredibly costly, and organizations do and should try to avoid them. But careful supervision, resetting expectations and performance improvement plans can only go so far. Sometimes you simply have the wrong person in the job.

Reassigning or removing an employee is tough. I've never met a leader who enjoys this or takes it lightly. I also know from experience, having been on either end of that conversation more than once. I'd given my client a lot to think about.

COACHING PROMPTS:

- Are you avoiding making a decision because you will reverse a previous decision you've made, and others will know about the reversal?
- What are the costs of acting? Of not acting?

7

The road trip

Living on the East Coast with family in the Midwest for 20 years has meant *a lot* of cross-country road trips for my family and me.

I tend to gamify the drive time to keep myself from getting bored when I drive. If Waze says we're running 10 minutes behind or 10 minutes ahead compared to when we left, I try to figure out why. I think it's fascinating that making a 15-minute stop turns into a 45-minute delay.

So, I prefer to drive as fast as safely possible, and to stop as few times as we can manage. It makes for a shorter day. Of course, when you're traveling with another adult, a child and a dog, you've got four stomachs and bladders to think about.

I had a client who struggled to give her team positive reinforcement because it felt like breaking her stride. She was incredibly focused on results, and growth, to the detriment of the people side of her role. I asked her to

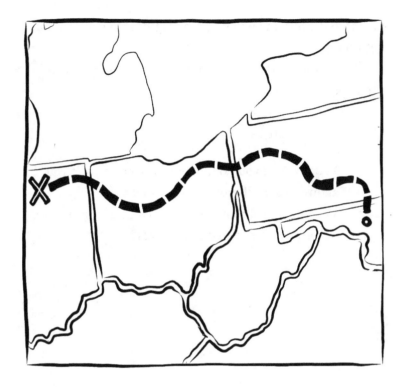

think about one of those cross-country road trips for a moment.

You can't stay alive without food, water and relieving yourself. Fighter pilots make arrangements to handle this sort of thing in the air, after all. So you can remain relentlessly focused on getting to your destination as quickly as possible, but that comes at the expense of comfort and sustenance for you and your passengers. Or you can pack snacks and drinks, and build in time for stretching and bathroom breaks a few times along the way. You can still give yourself an arrival deadline and try to beat it, but everyone will be in far better shape when you get there.

The detour isn't a distraction. It's a necessary part of the trip.

COACHING PROMPTS:

- What would you do more of for your team, if you allowed yourself more time to do it?
- When do results and efficiency come at the expense of something else that's important?

8

~∋

The elevator ride

Our social styles don't define who we are, but they define how we act. Are you outgoing or reserved? Do you see new interactions as more of an opportunity or a chore?

To illustrate this distinction, a client once conjured up the image of an elevator ride. What you do in that elevator showcases your social style.

You're not in a huge hurry. And you're not riding to your doctor's office to receive potentially devastating news. This is just an ordinary, workday elevator ride. (Pandemic note: let's assume it is once again safe to ride in elevators with other people.)

Do you say hello to everyone and strike up a conversation, missing your floor in the process? Or do you hit the fire alarm button when nobody's looking, so they all leave and you have an express ride to your destination? In other words, is your ideal elevator ride a journey full of potential connections or a short solo endeavor?

As an introvert, I'll smile and nod or say hello to keep it polite. Then I tend to stare at the floor and hope for as few stops as possible. I can't think of a single meaningful relationship in my life that has come as the result of the many hundreds of elevator rides I've taken. Yet it's entirely possible I missed some opportunities while I was quietly looking at my feet.

I love the idea of an elevator ride as an illustration of social styles, and also as an opportunity for trying on a different one. These experiences tend to be pretty short and pretty temporary, unless you're riding up dozens of floors in a skyscraper.

COACHING PROMPTS:

- What do you know about your social style and when it comes into play?
- How might you stretch yourself toward a different style through a small experiment or two?

9

⤳

Grandma's chocolate cake

My clients and I talk about delegation a lot. It's a tough topic for new managers, as they need to get used to watching people on their team do work that they, themselves, built a reputation on doing. For some more experienced leaders, it can be hard to let go. The end result is a sort of chilling effect on the team — they don't feel free to experiment, fail, grow and succeed.

I can relate. One of my jobs was as head of communications with a whole team of professionals behind me. The chief executive of our organization fancied himself the best writer in the building, so he would often line-edit individual pieces of copy. Leaving aside whether this was a wise use of his scarce time and attention, it left no room for the rest of us to maneuver.

How to get around this? I ask clients to think about what would happen if they wanted to put a member of their team in charge of dessert.

You could hand over Grandma's family chocolate cake recipe and carefully review the ingredients one by one. You could stand in the kitchen and demonstrate where all of the utensils and bakeware are to be found — and where they should go back once the project is over. You could even hold the measuring cups and pour the flour and sugar.

If you do all of these things, you will feel useful. You will also, almost certainly, receive a version of your grandmother's chocolate cake on time and up to your standards.

But what will your budding pastry chef employee learn through this experience? Will they be able to produce something delicious the next time you're not in the kitchen?

Consider telling your staffer this instead: "You're responsible for having dessert on my desk at 9 a.m. Tuesday. I'm here if you have any questions or want to check in along the way."

In this scenario, it is almost certain you will not get Grandma's chocolate cake. You might receive a pizza. You might receive something completely inedible, or nothing at all. You might also get something that blows your taste buds away.

What does your team member get? Autonomy. The ability to take a risk and try something new, knowing it's safe if it doesn't work out completely the first time. And maybe, just maybe, ownership over a new creation that you helped inspire into being.

COACHING PROMPTS:

- What can you delegate in a way that allows for creativity, exploration or even failure?
- What risks are you trying to avoid? What opportunities might present themselves?

10

〜

The frozen shoulder

I'm lying on my side on a vinyl-covered table, under fluorescent lights. I'm huffing and puffing a bit under the strain of my assigned task: rotate my right arm backwards, with a two-pound dumbbell in my hand. By the middle of the third set, it might as well have been 100 pounds. I just can't move it anymore.

I'd really rather be anywhere else, doing anything else.

The physical therapist is kind and encouraging. She notes the progress I've made in the last week or two, sends me away with a new take-home exercise and wishes me well.

And it's my experience in trying to recover from a frozen shoulder since January — with PT, massage, acupuncture and all manner of topical creams — that has me thinking about the power of positive feedback.

I've written before about how a few small words can make a big impact. Today, I'm thinking about a client who told me recently that he struggles with praise. It is an

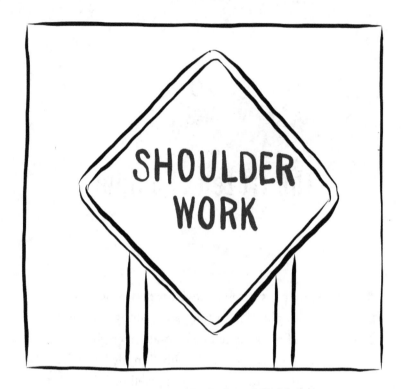

expected component of leadership at his company, but he gets frustrated by mistakes and doesn't want to hand out participation trophies.

I've realized two things through my PT experience:

1. Progress requires recognition.
2. Progress looks different for everyone.

This is the first physical therapist I've ever visited. Among the things I've learned as we talked during our sessions is that she does Olympic weightlifting for fun when she's not seeing patients. In other words, the person charged with helping me be able to lift both arms above my head again… could easily lift me over her head.

I was definitely a bit self-conscious about struggling to do a single push-up or move a light resistance band. But then I realized it's not her job to compare me to herself or anyone else. It's her job to compare me to me.

And so it goes in leadership as well. When we are charged with helping people on our teams grow, we meet them where they are and work from there. It's less important where we were ourselves when we were in a similar role in our careers. When they progress, we rejoice.

The words of encouragement from my therapist matter for a different reason, as do her numerical observations of how my range of motion is improving. It's hard for me to see and feel the progress because I've been living with this situation every day. She takes snapshots over time. Hearing that I'm actually getting somewhere is very reassuring. It keeps me motivated to do the home exercises and to see myself beating this someday.

COACHING PROMPTS:

- What progress are you noticing among members of your team?
- What habits can you develop toward acknowledging and praising that progress regularly?

11

The helicopter manager

I'd been working with a client at a large firm for about a year. Now, thanks to a shift in management priorities, she was going to head a new signature initiative. She was also moving away from her existing team.

My client had suspected for several months that this move was coming. She thought the world of her team members, having hand-selected several of them. Still, she couldn't shake the feeling that they weren't prepared for the transition that was about to happen. This concern was keeping her from focusing on the new assignment herself.

Perhaps fresh from another day of pandemic-parenting a toddler while working from home, she came to a realization.

"I've been tying their shoes for them for too long. I've been a helicopter manager!"

Like many highly successful employees who climb the leadership ladder, my client had made a reputation as a skilled doer — among the firm's executives and its clients

too. She had recruited well and built out a business function to lead, helping her folks navigate an economic downturn and a confusing return-to-office policy. But she continued to find herself spending far too much time in the weeds. As a result, the staff hadn't grown in their roles as much as she had grown in hers.

It was time to make a change, because the transition meant my client now had a deadline in front of her. She resolved to have handoff conversations with each of her directs, making herself available for questions only once in a while after her shift into her new role. She seemed confident that they'd learn the ropes quickly once left alone to do so.

COACHING PROMPTS:

- How has a desire for perfection, or to protect your own reputation, kept you involved too directly in your team's work?
- What are a few ways you can begin to let go of this involvement?

SECTION 5

Transitions

As this book goes to press, we seem to be in the midst of a large global transition. Adapting to an unprecedented health crisis, shifting to remote work and grappling with conflicting life priorities has led millions of people to seek transitions. Work will simply never be the same, for better or for worse.

Think of the transition into a different role within the same organization. Or a new workplace after many years with the same employer. Or a retirement. Most of us will experience transitions like these at least once within a career. I had more than a dozen jobs before starting my own coaching practice, which was an extraordinary change. It's also a change that seems more appealing to some than to others.

I spend a lot of time coaching leaders through various transitions. The following pages are filled with analogies on how to think about and how to navigate them.

1

~⚯

The robot vacuum career path

For nearly 20 years, the robot vacuum cleaner has delighted its users and their guests by — I suppose — bringing a little unpredictability and intrigue into the mundane: vacuuming. I don't own one, and I remain surprised that there is enough of a market out there among people who prefer to avoid vacuuming manually. But the indefatigable giant hockey puck contraption is really useful to me for another reason: it's the perfect analogy for my own career and that of many others I've coached.

What's your career path? What's your vision? What's your 5-year plan? I haven't had good answers to these questions in decades. If I had followed my original thinking on this front, I might have ended up a car designer, an astronaut or the Generation X answer to Bill Kurtis or Peter Jennings. None of these things happened.

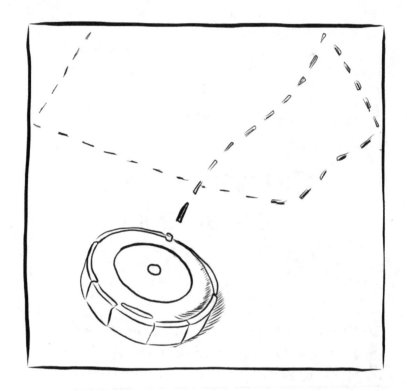

Instead, I followed my gut from opportunity to opportunity. I found success in discovering where I could learn and grow, and how this growth could carry me along to the next thing. This is how I went from television reporter and anchor to executive coach over the course of a couple of decades, with many stops along the way. It was definitely deliberate. It may have been strategic. And it was definitely not a path, a line or an arc.

My career squiggle is where the robot vacuum comes back into our conversation. It does what it is supposed to do, happily bopping along on its assigned mission of removing dust and cat hair from the floor. Then it hits an obstacle. It changes directions and repeats the same set of steps. After a number of minutes or hours, it has succeeded in the task of vacuuming the place. It hasn't followed anything resembling a straight line or even a series of straight lines.

I believe there is value in foresight and value in planning. The best leaders are able to do this for entire organizations, and their ability to do so sets them apart. Sticking devoutly to a plan that follows a straight line, on the other hand, can hamper creativity and stifle innovation. It's not a good way to make the magic happen.

I'll never retire with a gold watch after decades of service with the same employer, let alone in the same occupation or industry. But I wouldn't trade my career squiggle either.

Coaching prompts:

- In what way might following a pre-determined path be holding you back?
- What can you do to equip yourself to recognize opportunities in the future, especially unconventional ones?

2

Gov. Edgar in the back seat

Governor Jim Edgar was an Illinois politician known as a capable man with a less-than-magnetic personality. I was a young TV reporter in 1999 when Gov. Edgar gave his last round of interviews before leaving office.

I'm quite sure now that he used the exact same line with a dozen other reporters, and that a staffer wrote it for him. But I still remember it decades later: "I'll know I'm not governor anymore when I get in the backseat of a car and it doesn't go anywhere."

It was an elected official's apt reflection on returning to private life after more than three decades in the public eye. He would go from being responsible for a multibillion-dollar budget and tens of thousands of employees to being a college professor.

For most of us, no transition will be quite as dramatic as this. Yet we would all be wise to think about what

we're about to give up and what we're about to gain in a transition.

When I left television news not long after Gov. Edgar's retirement, I became a former reporter and anchor. I thought I would miss having important people return my phone calls. I later discovered I don't like talking on the phone that much. My station gave me a $500 a year clothing allowance, a princely sum for a guy in his early 20s. But it wasn't long before I made enough money to buy my own clothes, and I was in my 40s before I decided not to wear ties for work anymore.

Preparation makes any transition more successful, and a lot of that preparation is mental. It can help us decide whether certain trade-offs are worth the trouble, and help us adjust to the new stage when the transition is complete.

COACHING PROMPTS:

- What are three elements of your current role that you'd miss most if you had a different role?
- How can you prepare to replace those elements yourself in a new situation?

3

⟿

Buying a new house

Many of my clients bring their job searches into the Zoom box opposite me. I've had the benefit of their collective wisdom and more than a dozen jobs myself. It's an exercise that forces your brain into a sort of multiverse: you imagine your life in a number of different possibilities at once. What I've learned from this process is that there's no such thing as The One.

There is no single position that is the best fit for you across all of space and time.

Are there careers, or even jobs, that can last for all of a person's working days? Sure. You can also think you're in one of those when you're not. This has happened to me more than once.

Finding a new job is a lot like buying a house.

Buying a house is rarely something people do often. It can have major consequences for your quality of life, and for your family's quality of life. It has a major impact on your

finances. And all manner of considerations go into this kind of a decision.

Far too many variables go into the process of buying a house for The One to be possible. It's a product of what you decide you must have, what you can live with and live without, how much money you're prepared to spend *and when you're looking to purchase.*

Leaving aside the bonkers real estate market in many major metropolitan areas, this simply means you will end up with an entirely different house on your hands than if you went hunting 6 months ago or 6 months from now. You may also end up deciding to stay where you live now.

So it is with job hunting. It depends on all of the variables on your list, plus the timing. Some elements of timing are within your control and others are not. Once you've made the decision to leap, you do yourself a disservice by wondering what if. It's time to make that job your own, much like you'd be painting rooms or hanging new drapes.

COACHING PROMPTS:

- Which elements of the job search process can you control? Which ones can you not control?
- What can you do to let go of other possibilities that existed before you made your decision?

4

I won the election

I'd been looking forward to this coaching session. The client was a rising star in his own company and had agreed to an interview with a potential employer. It was an opportunity he hadn't sought, brought to him by a friend of his. He'd been excited about the possibilities when we'd talked them through on our last call.

We said our Zoom hellos and got into the discussion. I was mostly in listening mode. As he recounted the events of the past few days, he seemed pretty mellow. The tone didn't match the substance. He'd come up with a list of things he might want out of a new position, and the company had agreed to almost everything on it! He could build his own team and advance the cause of racial equity in his field. He could work from anywhere and would receive a big salary and title bump for his trouble.

Finally, I offered an observation. "I have to say, as you're telling me this story, your energy isn't leaping out of the screen at me."

He told me he hadn't thought of it until now, but the situation seemed weighty in addition to exciting. He'd have to talk to his current leadership about it. And if he accepted, he'd have to stretch into the role he had successfully made the case to undertake.

"I can understand where you are in your head about this," I said. "Imagine you've been elected President of the United States for the first time. The endless campaigning, all the travel, all the supporters. You've been questing for this thing for so long. And now you actually have to govern."

You have to go do the thing. It requires a different set of skills and a different team of players than the quest required.

It's going to be harder and often less exciting. And sustaining one's energy and momentum often requires recapturing a little bit of that campaign excitement from time to time.

COACHING PROMPTS:

- How might your excitement for a potential transition seem less exciting because of the seriousness and difficulty of the role you would take on?
- In what ways can you recapture some of your initial enthusiasm and take it with you along the way?

5

What's in your backpack?

At the time of this writing, the working world seems in the midst of a giant upheaval. It's a flurry of career changes, retirements, cross-country moves... all as the administrators among us try to figure out if, how and when to get employees back into their offices. A lot of folks are moving around, and they're seeking my support to get ready.

I've asked my clients to imagine that a job or career change is like making an international move. You know that you can't take everything with you, and you shouldn't try to do that anyway. You need to account for the climate, the type of housing and what you'll be doing with your time in the new place as you make these decisions. And you'll need to put a few things in your backpack for the long flight to your new country of residence.

So it is when you're seeking a new work situation. You will fill your backpack with the things about your job, or your

career, that are most important to you. You're most effective when you have them, and you'll use them right away and often. Think about stature within the organization, span of control, access to resources, the type of work itself.

Things you still need that don't belong in the backpack will make their way to you eventually. The movers will bring them, or they'll end up in a shipping container. But there's one more category of items to consider before you pack anything. What goes in the garbage bin behind the building right away, without a second thought?

The list of discards for a move is your ketchup packets, your old magazines, your outfits that you never wore and never want to see again. So, what about your professional discards? You don't want to work on, think about or be responsible for these things anymore. Knowing what they are will help you figure out what you want to do next.

Coaching prompts:

- What are the must-haves for your next work adventure? Why are they must-haves?
- What are you eager to discard from your current work situation? Why?

6

⌁

Selling off the furniture

Several calls before, my client told me of her plans to retire in a few months. (She became the latest of many to tell me about new directions in their career paths in 2021.) But it was something she tossed out during the first few minutes of this call that really made me think.

The retirement would also bring a downsizing from a large house into something more fitting for a pair of empty-nesters. So my client and her husband were in the process of deciding which furniture to sell. I realized she was in the midst of two pretty similar processes at the same time.

When you're leaving your job to retire, or to move on to something new, you've got a bunch of stuff you just don't need anymore. (We covered packing your backpack in the previous analogy.) Not everything fits. Now you're beginning to transfer ownership of those things to someone who can benefit from them more than you can.

Institutional memory, contact files, lists of procedures, retelling of experiences. These are all things you leave behind

to your team or your successor. Then there's the drop-leaf table and all the chairs, along with the service for 12. If your new life is going to be more breakfast nook than dining room, you've got some unloading to do.

COACHING PROMPTS:

- What would be most useful for your team or your successor to know before you leave?
- If you eased yourself down to making no contribution whatsoever on your last day of the job, what would that look like?

SECTION 6

Coaching

Coaching is a powerful modality that helps leaders grow. I believe in it because I've been through it. There is a straight line between what I do for a living now and the discoveries I made during my work with my very first coach, Jessica Bronzert of the Sparks Group.

It is certainly possible to achieve growth on one's own. Tens of thousands of books and countless on-demand training programs help make it so. But one-on-one coaching is a catalyst that makes the process stronger and faster.

Coaches provide four distinct advantages over a self-service approach:

- Curation. Coaches know how to find the best resources on specific topics, and how to help these resonate with their clients.

- Reframing. Coaches help their clients see challenges through a new lens. The collection you're now reading is 52 examples of this reframing.
- Accountability. Coaches create action plans with their clients and will follow up to make sure the actions happen. Holding the client accountable makes it stick.
- Challenge. Coaches don't accept the first answer or the most obvious one. If something doesn't make sense, or sounds like an excuse, they'll name it when few others in a leader's life are likely to do so.

This book originated from my coaching practice, and it wouldn't be complete without at least a couple of analogies about coaching itself. Here they are.

1

The 5 a.m. winter run

I like to say that I have a pretty serious running habit. I have been running 5 half-marathons a year for the past several years, and my Sundays don't feel right without a long run in the morning. Even still, I just don't feel like doing it sometimes.

So I naturally leaned forward in my chair when a client and I were discussing accountability and she laid this one on me: "It's easier to go out for that 5 a.m. run when it's 30 degrees outside if someone else is waiting to go with you."

Yes indeed. Part of the magic of coaching is accountability. It is easier to do hard things, especially hard things that lead to lasting change, if someone is holding you accountable for doing them. My clients commit to taking actions, and I'll ask them about those actions during the next session or several. Accountability works.

I've used it in my own practice by assigning myself deadlines and communicating those deadlines to others, so

I have someone other than myself counting on completion. You are reading these words because I asked a group of coaches to be my accountability partners on completing the book.

Even though the client's analogy resonated with me, I run more than 90 percent of my miles by myself. As an introvert, I value the solitude and the fact that it's an individual sport.

But accountability is in fact one of the reasons I run races. I like to imagine that the hundreds or thousands of other runners are counting on me showing up and delivering my best performance. In a way, that's part of our accountability to one another.

Coaching prompts:

- How can a coach, a mentor, a boss or a colleague support you with accountability on a challenge you're facing?
- How can you help hold someone else accountable for a challenge they are facing?

2

Jigsaw puzzle session

I love a good jigsaw puzzle. In fact, I probably put together a couple of puzzles a month on average when many of us were spending more time at home during the pandemic. It's a physically tangible process. It can be done a little or a lot at a time. It is a creation, yet a temporary one that involves someone else's vision. And by swapping finished puzzles with friends and family, and making good use of thrift stores, it's a hobby that doesn't cost a lot of money or drain the planet of resources.

Some puzzlers are meticulous in their preparation. They'll spend hours turning over all of the pieces and sorting by color or shape before they even start assembling. Yet even as a generally methodical and tidy person myself, I never do this. I like to dive right into a box of unsorted, unflipped pieces and make sense of the chaos.

This is also one of my favorite ways to hold a coaching session.

If a client comes into their assigned time without a clear agenda, or without a clear starting or ending point, I encourage them to dump the puzzle pieces on the table instead. We'll spend the hour sorting and flipping ideas. We'll start spotting connections and themes, and explore them together. It's quite impossible to build a large and complicated puzzle within the course of a single hour, so we might take something small (say, 100 pieces) and resolve it, or start the process on something more ambitious (1,000 pieces or more) and return to it the next time.

Unlike an actual jigsaw puzzle, the puzzle coaching session can yield surprising results. There's no picture on the box. You might think you were assembling a picture of Venice, and end up with a spice cabinet or a montage of kittens.

But who doesn't love an unexpected montage of kittens?

Coaching prompts:

- How might you draw connections among seemingly random thoughts in your head?
- Can a thought partner help you sort and connect, leaving a clearer picture more quickly?

3

~⊃

The TV series

A great television series holds our interest because of a long-running plotline or story arc. How will the characters resolve their conflicts? Who will end up as a couple? What happens if one of them decides to leave the show?

Week by week, or even more than once a day if we're binging, we develop relationships with the characters on our favorite shows.

And every once in a while, the producers will throw in an episode that could air at any point during the season. It doesn't advance the overall storyline. It may take place in an unusual location — think office party or class field trip. But it's interesting because it's different, and it still deepens our understanding of the characters. The party ends or the bus returns to school. We're usually back to business with the next episode.

Coaching sessions can work this way too.

We usually work according to a short list of major themes the client has identified in their work life. Think executive presence, delegation, difficult conversations. Most sessions hit one or two of these themes and keep the engagement moving along an arc. At the end of the arc, we find progress or even resolution. The coach and the client deepen their relationship with each other through this process.

And sometimes we have a one-off session. These don't contain any discussion of the major themes. Instead, it's the terrible meeting that happened 5 minutes before the coaching call. It's the preparation for a meeting in front of important stakeholders. The run-up to an annual performance review, either given or received.

In the one-offs, it's still possible to advance our progress along that engagement arc. The coach ends up with a stronger understanding of the client and context around that person. And we typically return to the usual theme-oriented session next time.

COACHING PROMPTS:

- What are the major themes you're working through in your work life right now?
- When was the last time you had a situation in which a one-off coaching session would have been helpful?

Artwork Attributions

Running past a bicycle is adapted from a photo by Ian Donaldson and used under the Creative Commons Attribution-Share Alike 3.0 Unported license. https://creativecommons.org/licenses/by-sa/3.0/deed.en

The boulder and the forklift is adapted from a photo by Compliance and Safety, http://complianceandsafety.com/blog/photo-realistic-forklift-illustration-free-stock-photo-under-creative-commons-license/ and used under the Creative Commons Attribution-Share Alike 3.0 Unported license. https://creativecommons.org/licenses/by-sa/3.0/deed.en

You're not a bus is adapted from a photo by Swagging and used under the Creative Commons Attribution-Share Alike 4.0 International license. https://creativecommons.org/licenses/by-sa/4.0/deed.en

Don't wash the rental car is adapted from a photo by NeONBRAND on Unsplash.

The 5 a.m. winter run is adapted from a photo by Vincent Desjardins and used under the Creative Commons Attribution 2.0 Generic license. https://creativecommons.org/licenses/by/2.0/

Author photograph is adapted from a photo by Jenifer Morris Photography and used by permission.

Author's Acknowledgments

I tend to learn by doing, and what you have in your hands is the product of my latest and greatest learning experience. An early and valuable lesson is how much of a village it takes to make a book.

Thanks to my various clients who came up with analogies and allowed me to use or modify them. Thanks to Mike Jelen for keeping me honest about how bridges are built.

I am grateful to Dennis Samson for his inspired cover art. We've worked together on projects large and small for more than a decade. His ability to pull a jumble of thoughts into a visually appealing piece still inspires me after all of those years.

I also owe a hearty thanks to Dr. Maura Grace Harrington Logue for editing these words and to Andrea Reider for uniting them with the illustrations in book form.

To my family for sticking with me as I attempted to make the outlandish possible, thank you.

And to L, my life partner for more than a quarter century and now my creative partner, much gratitude and even more love.

About the Author

Alan Heymann is a leadership and executive coach, specializing in helping his fellow introverts find their superpowers, and in working with leaders in transition. Through his practice, Peaceful Direction, Alan has coached leaders born in 19 countries who work on 5 continents.

Alan has a Bachelor of Science in Journalism from Northwestern University, a Juris Doctorate from The George Washington University Law School and an Executive Certificate in Leadership Coaching from Georgetown University. He is on the Board of Trustees of the Barker Adoption Foundation. He's followed a plant-based diet since 2002 and enjoys running half marathons. He and his family live in Maryland.

About the Illustrator

L indy Russell-Heymann is an elementary school art teacher with more than two decades of experience in education and the arts. She began her career as a theatrical costume designer before becoming a teacher. She is a winner of the "Power of Art" award from the Robert Rauschenberg Foundation.

Lindy has a Bachelor of Fine Arts from DePaul University and a Master of Arts in Art Education from The Ohio State University. She's followed a plant-based diet since 2002 and enjoys working with stained and fused glass. She and her family live in Maryland.

CPSIA information can be obtained
at www.ICGtesting.com
Printed in the USA
BVHW050319100122
625856BV00002B/84